SPECTRUM®
READERS

LEVEL 1

BUSY!
Insects

By Lisa Kurkov

Carson-Dellosa
Publishing

D1059586

An imprint of Carson-Dellosa Publishing, LLC
P.O. Box 35665
Greensboro, NC 27425-5665

carsondellosa.com

Printed in the USA. All rights reserved.
ISBN 978-1-4838-0114-8

01-002141120

Insects have six legs.
They hatch from eggs.
Their bodies have three parts.
They have no backbones.
Busy insects are everywhere!

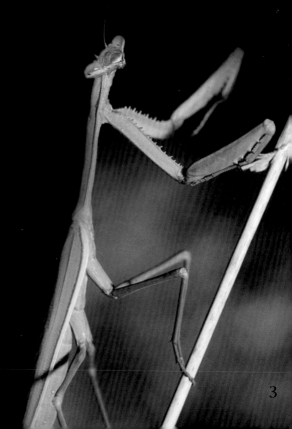

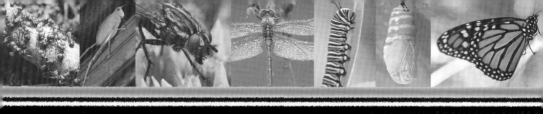

Cicada

Busy cicadas make a
loud humming noise.
Some can be heard a
mile away!

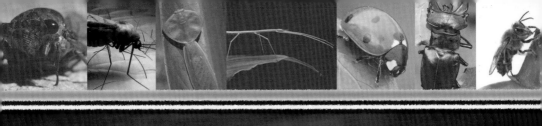

Mosquito

Busy mosquitoes feed on blood.
They leave behind an itchy, red bump.

Leaf Mantis

Busy leaf mantises
hide on plants.
Predators will not
spot them.

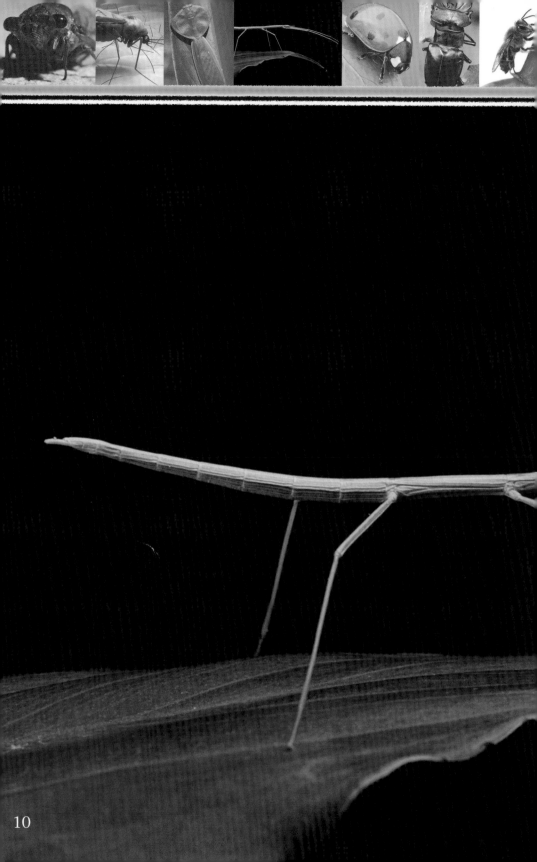

Stick Insect

Busy stick insects
pretend to be twigs.
One kind is almost
two feet long!

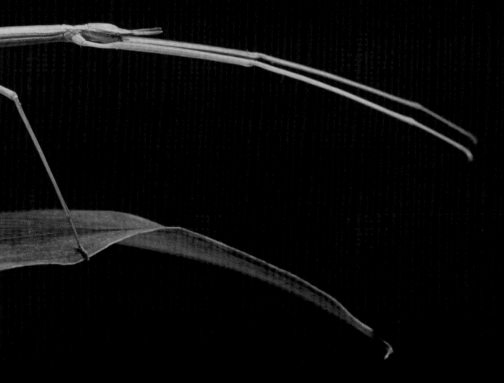

Ladybug

Busy ladybugs eat insects
that harm plants.
They help protect plants
in a farmer's field.

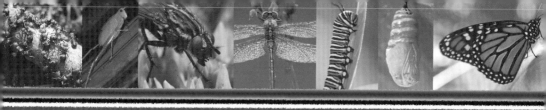

Stag Beetle

Busy stag beetles use their jaws to fight. Their big jaws look like antlers.

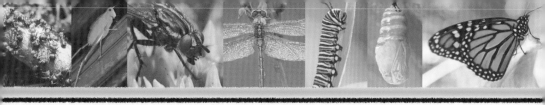

Bee

Busy bees carry pollen from flower to flower. They help fruits and vegetables grow.

Ants

Busy ants have many jobs to do.
They find food, make nests, and lay eggs.

Grasshopper

Busy grasshoppers jump
in the grass.
Some can leap almost
two feet!

Fly

Busy flies search for food outside and inside.
They use their feet to taste!

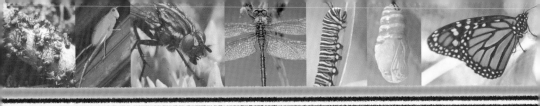

Dragonfly

Busy dragonflies hover over
ponds and streams.
They can fly backward
like helicopters!

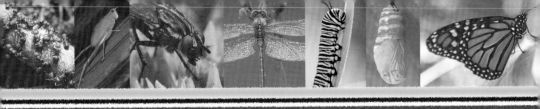

Monarch Caterpillar

Busy caterpillars munch leaves. They store energy to get ready for a big change.

Monarch Chrysalis

Busy chrysalises
(KRIS uh lis ses) have wiggly
caterpillars inside.
Soon, a butterfly will
emerge.

Monarch Butterfly

Busy monarch butterflies
fly long distances.
In the fall, they travel
to Mexico!

BUSY! Insects
Comprehension Questions

1. What are three things insects have in common?

2. What do mosquitoes eat?

3. What helps a leaf mantis and stick insect hide?

4. How do ladybugs help people?

5. How does a stag beetle use its jaws?

6. Why are bees so important?

7. Where do dragonflies live?

8. How far can a grasshopper jump?

9. What part of its body does a fly use to taste?

10. What is a chrysalis?

11. Where do monarchs go when it gets cold outside?